GENDER VIOLENCE

a development and human

rights issue

by

Charlotte Bunch

and

Roxanna Carrillo

Charlotte Bunch, US feminist organiser and editor since 1968, is the author of numerous essays including her latest collection *Passionate Politics: Feminist Theory in Action.* She has been working on issues of global feminism for over a decade and is currently Director of the Centre for Women's Global Leadership at Douglass College, Rutgers University in New Jersey.

Roxanna Carrillo, a Peruvian feminist who has been active in the women's movement in her country, is currently living in New York where she works at the United Nations Development Fund for Women (UNIFEM). She wrote this paper while at the Centre for Women's Global Leadership at Rutgers University, where she is also a doctoral student in Political Science.

This is a shortened version of 'Gender Violence: A Development and Human Rights Issue' originally published by the Centre for Women's Global Leadership, Rutgers University, New Brunswick, New Jersey, USA, 1991.

This pamphlet is published with the assistance of the Council of Women's Aid, Dublin.

First published in Ireland in 1992 by
Attic Press
4 Upper Mount Street
Dublin 2

British Library Cataloguing in Publication Data
Bunch, Charlotte
    Gender Violence: Development and Human Rights Issue.
    - (LIP Pamphlets Series)
    I. Title II. Carrillo Roxanna
    III. Series
    305.3

ISBN 1-85594-033-7

Cover Design: Paula Nolan
Typesetting: Attic Press
Printing: Elo Press

FOREWORD

Ireland is a country which is perceived as having an excellent record on human rights. This pamphlet challenges the government of Ireland to recognise violence against women as a breach of human rights, given the huge, as yet undocumented, problem which violence against women has become.

In Ireland, violence against women has traditionally been perceived as a family/cultural/personal problem. This has resulted in a deafening silence and a trivialising of the issue so that few state resources have been allocated either to research the problem or to adequately respond to the needs of the victim. Seeing violence against women as a violation of human rights places responsibility for its eradication firmly in the hands of the state, thus removing it from the 'private' into the 'public' world. This shift of emphasis implies that legislation, police enforcement, education and the necessary services to meet the needs of the victims must all be provided by the state.

The experience of Women's Aid has been that women who come to refuges have usually been severely beaten, punched and kicked, sustaining serious injuries, ranging from cuts and bruising to broken bones and internal damage. Such physical abuse is always accompanied by mental, verbal, economic and sexual abuse.

State responsibility must be assumed in an area where there are voluntary groups such as Women's Aid, Rape Crisis Centres, and other refuges, struggling to meet the needs of a small proportion of victims. These organisations use their scarce resources in crisis intervention, with little or no support from the state. They experience extreme difficulty in addressing seriously the causes and possible prevention of the continually escalating problem of violence against women.

By examining the issue on a global level it becomes clear that tradition, culture and religion are very often used to justify and propagate violent practices against women. The resistance in Ireland to lifting the lid on domestic violence is hugely contributed to by the mythology surrounding the sacredness of 'family' life, ignoring the fact that the family can be a very dangerous place for women and children. Many women who find themselves in a violent situation are discouraged from taking action to protect themselves and/or their children because of the pressure on them to 'keep the family together'.

In Ireland, the silence surrounding the issue of violence against women is clearly demonstrated by a serious lack of statistical data. The

3

few raw statistics available are chilling. Gardai in Dublin report that, in a four month period, in 1991, they answered 1,568 calls for help in domestic violence situations. Recent research on homelessness in Dublin (Kellegher, Kellegher and McCarthy, 1992) has highlighted the frightening lack of refuge space available to abused women and their children: 55 women with 112 children sought refuge from domestic violence in a three week period, in 1991, in Dublin. They did not receive it. All 20 refuge spaces in the city were already taken. The British Home Office report of 1976 recommends that one refuge space should be provided to every 10,000 of the population. We have 20 *suitable* refuge spaces for one million inhabitants in Dublin city!

Global data shows that violence against women is not a class indicated issue. However, the economic dependency of women is undoubtedly a huge factor in preventing them from leaving a situation of violence. As Charlotte Bunch and Roxanna Carrillo argue, one cannot address violence against women in isolation. It must be done within the framework of a documented critique of the political, cultural and socio-economic position of women in society. Such a critique is fundamental and must be the first step to be taken by policy makers and legislators if Irish women are to believe that there is a genuine commitment to end this war on women which sees them battered and murdered in their own homes in Ireland today.

Monica O'Connor
Women's Aid
Dublin 1992

Monica O'Connor has been actively involved in the Irish women's movement for the past ten years, working on issues of poverty, education and violence against women.

WOMEN'S RIGHTS AS HUMAN RIGHTS

toward a re-vision of human rights

Charlotte Bunch

Significant numbers of the world's population are routinely subject to torture, starvation, terrorism, humiliation, mutilation, and even murder simply because they are female. Crimes such as these against any group other than women would be recognised as a civil and political emergency as well as a gross violation of the victim's humanity. Yet, despite a clear record of deaths and demonstrable abuse, women's rights are not commonly classified as human rights. This is problematic both theoretically and practically, because it has grave consequences for the way society views and treats the fundamental issues of women's lives.

Women's human rights are violated in a variety of ways. Of course, women sometimes suffer abuses such as political repression in ways that are similar to abuses suffered by men. In these situations, female victims are often invisible because the dominant image of the political actor in our world is male. However, many violations of women's human rights are distinctly connected to being female - that is, women are discriminated against and abused on the basis of gender. Women also experience sexual abuse in situations where their other human rights are being violated, as political prisoners or members of persecuted ethnic groups, for example. In this paper I address those abuses in which gender is a primary or related factor because gender-related abuse has been most neglected and offers the greatest challenge to the field of human rights today.

The concept of human rights is one of the few moral visions ascribed to internationally. Although its scope is not universally agreed upon, it strikes deep chords of response among many. Promotion of human rights is a widely accepted goal and thus provides a useful framework for seeking redress of gender abuse. Further, it is one of the few concepts that speaks to the need for trans-national activism and concern about the lives of people globally. *The Universal Declaration of Human Rights* adopted in 1948 symbolises this world vision and defines human rights broadly. While not much is said about women, Article 2 does entitle all to *'the rights and freedoms set forth in this Declaration, without distinction of any kind, such as race, colour, sex, language, religion, political or other opinion, national or social origin, property, birth or other status.'*

Since 1948, the world community has continuously debated varying interpretations of human rights in response to global developments. Little of this discussion, however, has addressed questions of gender, and only recently have significant challenges been made to a vision of human rights which excludes much of women's experiences. The concept of human rights, like all vibrant visions, is not static or the property of any one group; rather its meaning expands as people reconceive of their needs and hopes in relation to it. In this spirit, feminists redefine human rights abuses to include the degradation and violation of women. The specific experiences of women must be added to traditional approaches to human rights in order to make women more visible and to transform the concept and practice of human rights in our culture so that it takes better account of women's lives.

BEYOND RHETORIC: POLITICAL IMPLICATIONS

Few governments exhibit more than token commitment to women's equality as a basic human right in domestic or foreign policy. No government determines its policies toward other countries on the basis of their treatment of women, even when some aid and trade decisions are said to be based on a country's human rights record. Among non-governmental organisations, women are rarely a priority, and Human Rights Day programmes on 10 December seldom include discussion of issues like violence against women or reproductive rights. When it is suggested that governments and human rights organisations should respond to women's rights as concerns that deserve such attention, a number of excuses are offered for why this cannot be done. The responses tend to follow one or more of these lines: (1) sex discrimination is too trivial, or not as important, or will come after larger issues of survival that require more serious attention; (2) abuse of women, while regrettable, is a cultural, private, or individual issue and not a political matter requiring state action; (3) while appropriate for other action, women's rights are not human rights per se; or (4) when the abuse of women is recognised, it is called inevitable or so pervasive that consideration of it is futile or will overwhelm other human rights questions. It is important to challenge these responses.

The narrow definition of human rights, recognised by many in the West as solely a matter of state violation of civil and political liberties, impedes consideration of women's rights.

6

Some important aspects of women's rights do fit into a civil liberties framework, but much of the abuse of women is part of a larger socio-economic web that entraps women, making them vulnerable to abuses which cannot be delineated as exclusively political or solely caused by states. The inclusion of 'second generation' or socio-economic human rights to food, shelter, and work - which are clearly delineated as part of the Universal Declaration of Human Rights - is vital to addressing women's concerns fully. Further, the assumption that states are not responsible for most violations of women's rights ignores the fact that abuses, although committed perhaps by private citizens, are often condoned or sanctioned by states. I will return to the question of state responsibility after responding to other instances of resistance to women's rights as human rights.

The most insidious myth about women's rights is that they are trivial or secondary to the concerns of life and death. Nothing could be farther from the truth; sexism kills. There is increasing documentation of the many ways in which being female is life-threatening. The following are a few examples:

- *Before birth:* Amniocentesis is used for sex selection leading to the abortion of more female fetuses at rates as high as 99 per cent in Bombay; in China and India, the two most populous nations, more males are born than females even though natural birth ratios would produce more females (Patel, 1987; Heise, 1989).
- *During childhood:* The World Health Organisation reports that in many countries, girls are fed less, breast fed for shorter periods of time, taken to doctors less frequently, and die or are physically and mentally maimed by malnutrition at higher rates than boys (Ravindran, 1986).
- *In adulthood:* The denial of women's rights to control their bodies in reproduction threatens women's lives, especially where this is combined with poverty and poor health services. In Latin America, complications from illegal abortions are the leading cause of death for women between the ages of fifteen and thirty-nine (Taylor, 1985).

Sex discrimination kills women daily. When combined with race, class, and other forms of oppression it constitutes a deadly denial of women's rights to life and liberty on a large scale throughout the world. The most pervasive violation of females is violence against women with its many manifestations from wife battery, incest, and rape, to dowry deaths, genital mutilation, and female sexual slavery. Some or all of these abuses occur in every country and are found in the home and in the work-place, on streets, campuses, and in prisons and refugee camps. They cross class, race, age, and national lines; and at the same time, the forms this violence takes often reinforce other oppressions such as racism, 'able-bodyism', and imperialism.

Even a short review of random statistics reveals that the extent of violence against women globally is staggering:

- In the United States, battery is the leading cause of injury to adult women, and a rape is committed every six minutes (Koop, 1989).

- In Peru 70 per cent of all crimes reported to police involve women who are beaten by their partners; and in Lima (a city of seven million people), 168,970 rapes were reported in 1987 alone (Portugal, 1988).

- In India, eight out of ten wives are victims of violence, either domestic battery, dowry-related abuse, or among the least fortunate, murder (Ashworth, 1989).

- In France, 95 per cent of the victims of violence are women; 51 per cent at the hands of a spouse or lover.

Violence against women is a touchstone that illustrates the limited concept of human rights and highlights the political nature of the abuse of women. As Lori Heise states: *'this is not random violence ... the risk factor is being female.'* Victims are chosen because of their gender. The message is domination: stay in your place or be afraid. Contrary to the argument that such violence is only personal or cultural, it is profoundly political. It results from the structural relationships of power, domination and privilege between men and women in society. Violence against women is central to maintaining those political relations at home, at work, and in all public spheres.

Failure to see the oppression of women as political also results in the exclusion of sex discrimination and violence against women from the human rights agenda. Female subordination runs so deep that it is still viewed as inevitable or natural, rather than seen as a politically constructed reality maintained by patriarchal interests, ideology, and institutions. But I do not believe that male violation of women is inevitable or natural. Such a belief requires a narrow and pessimistic view of men. If violence and domination are understood as a politically constructed reality, it is possible to imagine deconstructing that system and building more just interactions between the sexes.

The physical territory of this political struggle over what constitutes women's human rights is women's bodies. The importance of control over women can be seen in the intensity of resistance to laws and social changes that put control of women's bodies in women's hands: reproductive rights, freedom of sexuality whether heterosexual or lesbian, laws that criminalise rape in marriage, etc. Denial of

8

reproductive rights and homophobia are also political means of maintaining control over women and perpetuating sex roles and power which have human rights implications. The physical abuse of women is a reminder of this territorial domination and is sometimes accompanied by other forms of human rights abuse such as slavery (forced prostitution), sexual terrorism (rape), imprisonment (confinement to the home) or torture (systematic battery). Some cases are extreme, such as the women in Thailand who died in a brothel fire because they were chained to their beds. Most situations are more ordinary, like denying women decent education or jobs which leaves them prey to abusive marriages, exploitative work, and prostitution.

This raises once again the question of the state's responsibility for protecting women's human rights. Feminists have shown how the distinction between private and public abuse is a dichotomy often used to justify female subordination in the home. Riane Eisler argues that: *'the issue is what types of private acts are and are not protected by the right to privacy and/or the principle of family autonomy. Even more specifically, the issue is whether violations of human rights within the family such as genital mutilation, wife beating, and other forms of violence designed to maintain patriarchal control should be within the purview of human rights theory and action ... the underlying problem for human rights theory, as for most other fields of theory, is that the yardstick that has been developed for defining and measuring human rights has been based on the male as norm'* (Eisler, 1987).

The human rights community must move beyond its male defined norms in order to respond to the brutal and systematic violation of women globally. This does not mean that every human rights group must alter the focus of its work. However it does require examining patriarchal biases and acknowledging the rights of women as human rights. Governments must seek to end the politically and culturally constructed war on women rather than continue to perpetuate it. Every state has the responsibility to intervene in the abuse of women's rights within its borders and to end its collusion with the forces that perpetrate such violations in other countries.

TOWARD ACTION: PRACTICAL APPROACHES

The classification of human rights is more than just a semantics problem because it has practical policy consequences. Human rights are still considered to be more important than women's rights. The distinction perpetuates the idea that the rights of women are of a lesser order than the 'rights of man,' and as Eisler describes it, *'serves to justify practices that do not accord women full and equal status.* ' In the United Nations, the Human Rights Commission has more power to hear and investigate cases than the Commission on the Status of Women, more staff and budget, and better mechanisms for implementing its findings. Thus it makes a difference in what can be done if a case is deemed a violation of women's rights and not of human rights.

I have observed four basic approaches to linking women's rights to human rights. These approaches are presented separately here in order to identify each much more clearly. In practice, these approaches often overlap, and while each raises questions about the others, I see them as complementary. These approaches can be applied to many issues, but I will illustrate them primarily in terms of how they address violence against women in order to show the implications of their differences on a concrete issue.

1. Women's Rights as Political and Civil Rights. Taking women's specific needs into consideration as part of the already recognised 'first generation' human rights of political and civil liberties is the first approach. This involves both raising the visibility of women who suffer general human rights violations as well as calling attention to particular abuses women encounter because they are female. Thus, issues of violence against women are raised when they connect to other forms of violation. Groups like the women's task force of Amnesty International have taken this approach in pushing for Amnesty to launch a campaign on behalf of women political prisoners which would address the sexual abuse and rape of women in custody, their lack of maternal care in detention, and the resulting human rights abuse of their children.

The political and civil rights approach is a useful starting point for many human rights groups; by considering women's experiences, these groups can expand their efforts in areas where they are already working. This approach also raises contradictions that reveal the limits of a narrow civil liberties view. One contradiction is to define rape as a human rights abuse only when it occurs in state custody but not on the streets or in the home. Another is to say that a violation of the right to free speech occurs when someone is jailed for defending gay rights, but not when someone is jailed or even tortured and killed for homosexuality. Thus while this approach of adding women and stirring them into existing first generation human rights categories is useful, it is not enough by itself.

2. Women's Rights as Socio-economic Rights. The second approach includes the particular plight of women with regard to 'second generation' human rights such as the rights to food, shelter, health care,

10

and employment. This is an approach favoured by those who see the dominant Western human rights tradition and international law as too individualistic and identify women's oppression as primarily economic.

This tendency has its origins among socialists and labour activists who have long argued that political human rights are meaningless to many without economic rights as well. It focuses on the primacy of the need to end women's economic subordination as the key to other issues including women's vulnerability to violence. This particular focus has led to work on highlighting the feminisation of poverty, or what might better be called the increasing impoverishment of females. Poverty has not become strictly female, but females now comprise a higher percentage of the poor.

Looking at women's rights in the context of socio-economic development is another example of this approach. Third world peoples have called for an understanding of socio-economic development as a human rights issue. Within this demand, some have sought to integrate women into development and have examined women's specific needs in relation to areas like land ownership or access to credit. Among those working on women in development, there is growing interest in violence against women as both a health and development issue. If violence is seen as having negative consequences for social productivity, it may get more attention. This type of narrow economic measure, however, should not determine whether such violence is seen as a human rights concern. Violence as a development issue is linked to the need to understand development not just as an economic issue but also as a question of empowerment and human growth.

One of the limitations of this second approach has been its tendency to reduce women's needs to the economic sphere which implies that women's rights will follow automatically with third world development, which may involve socialism. This has not proven to be the case. Many working from this approach are no longer trying to add women into either the Western capitalist or socialist development models, but rather seek a transformative development process that links women's political, economic and cultural empowerment.

3. **Women's Rights and the Law.** The creation of new legal mechanisms to counter sex discrimination characterises the third approach to women's rights as human rights. These efforts seek to make existing legal and political institutions work for women and to expand the state's responsibility for the violation of women's human rights. National and local laws which address sex discrimination and violence against women are examples of this approach. These measures allow women to fight for their rights within the legal system. The

primary international illustration is the *Convention on the Elimination of All Forms of Discrimination Against Women.*

The Convention has been described as *'essentially an international bill of rights for women and a framework for women's participation in the development process ... (which) spells out internationally accepted principles and standards for achieving equality between women and men'* (IWRAW, 1988). Adopted by the UN General Assembly in 1979, the convention has been ratified or acceded to by 104 countries as of January, 1990. In theory these countries are obligated to pursue policies in accordance with it and to report on their compliance to the Committee on the Elimination of Discrimination Against Women (CEDAW).

While the Convention addresses many issues of sex discrimination, one of its shortcomings is failure to directly address the question of violence against women. CEDAW passed a resolution at its eighth session in Vienna in 1989 expressing concern that this issue be on its agenda and instructing states to include in their periodic reports information about statistics, legislation, and support services in this area. The Commonwealth Secretariat in its manual on the reporting process for the Convention also interprets the issue of violence against women as *'clearly fundamental to the spirit of the Convention,'* (1987) especially in Article 5 which calls for the modification of social and cultural patterns, sex roles and stereotyping, that are based on the idea of the inferiority or the superiority of either sex.

The Convention outlines a clear human rights agenda for women which, if accepted by governments, would mark an enormous step forward. It also carries the limitations of all such international documents in that there is little power to demand its implementation. Within the United Nations, it is not generally regarded as a convention with teeth, as illustrated by the difficulty that CEDAW has had in getting countries to report on compliance with its provisions. Further, it is still treated by governments and most non-governmental organisations as a document dealing with women's (read 'secondary') rights, not human rights. Nevertheless, it is a useful statement of principles endorsed by the United Nations around which women can organise to achieve legal and political change in their regions.

4. Feminist Transformation of Human Rights. Transforming the human rights concept from a feminist perspective, so that it will take greater account of women's lives, is the fourth approach. This approach raises the question of how women's rights relate to human rights by first looking at the violations of women's lives and asking how the human rights concept can be changed to be more responsive to women.

For example, the GABRIELA women's coalition in the Philippines simply stated that *'Women's Rights are Human Rights'* in launching a campaign last year. As Ninotchka Rosca explained, coalition members saw that *'human rights are not reducible to a question of legal and due process ... In the case of women, human rights are affected by the entire society's traditional perception of what is proper or not proper for women'* (Rosca, 1990). While work in the three previous approaches is often done from a feminist perspective, this last view is the most distinctly feminist with its woman-centred stance and refusal to wait for permission from some authority to determine what is or is not a human rights issue.

This transformative approach can be taken toward any issue, but those working from this approach have tended to focus most on abuses that arise specifically out of gender, such as reproductive rights, female sexual slavery, violence against women and 'family crimes' like forced marriage, compulsory heterosexuality, and female mutilation. These are also the issues most often dismissed as not really human rights questions. This is therefore the most hotly contested area and requires that barriers be broken down between public and private, state and non-governmental responsibilities.

The practical applications of transforming the human rights concept from feminist perspectives need to be explored further. The danger in pursuing this approach only is the tendency to become isolated from and competitive with other human rights groups because they have been so reluctant to address gender violence and discrimination. By recognising issues like violence against women as human rights concerns, human rights scholars and activists do not have to take these up as their primary tasks. However they do have to stop gate-keeping and guarding their prerogative to determine what is considered a 'legitimate' human rights issue.

All of these approaches contain aspects of what is necessary to achieve women's rights. At a time when dualist ways of thinking and views of competing economic systems are in question, the creative task is to look for ways to connect these approaches and to see how we can go beyond exclusive views of what people need in their lives. In the words of an early feminist group - we need bread and roses too. Women want food and liberty and the possibility of living lives of dignity, free from domination and violence. In this struggle, the recognition of women's rights as human rights can play an important role.

VIOLENCE AGAINST WOMEN

an obstacle to development

Roxanna Carrillo

Human development is a process of enlarging people's choices. The most critical of these wide-ranging choices are to live a long and healthy life, to be educated and to have access to resources needed for a decent standard of living. Additional choices include political freedom, guaranteed human rights and personal self-respect. Development enables people to have these choices.

UNDP, Human Development Report 1990.

The United Nations Decade for Women (1976-1985) helped to bring attention to the critical importance of women's activities for economic and social development. However, after fifteen years of efforts to integrate women into development, women are still only marginal beneficiaries of development programmes and policy goals. Various studies show that women remain in a disadvantaged position in employment, education, health, and government. There is no major field of activity and no country in which women have obtained equality with men.

In spite of the slow process of change, women working in the international development community have been successful in identifying issues critical for women's development that were not traditionally understood as central to the development process. One such area is gender violence. Violence against women was previously seen, if seen at all, as a private matter, a cultural and family issue, or at best, pertinent to social welfare policies. Those concerned with the general position of women have addressed gender violence within the framework of promoting peace and, increasingly, as part of the human rights agenda. These approaches underscore the multiple aspects of such violence but they in no way exhaust our understanding of the problem. There are still large gaps in our knowledge of the dimensions and effects of gender violence on the development process itself. Lack of statistical data is one of several problems in documenting the issue. We have reached a point where it is critical to understand how violence

14

as a form of control affects women's participation in the development process.

The emergence of violence as a crucial issue for third world women's development has occurred organically arising from grass roots women's endeavours, and has not been dictated by outside authorities or international agencies. For example, UNIFEM-funded projects from various regions of the world increasingly identify violence as a priority concern and/or as a problem that limits women's participation in development projects or their capacity to benefit from them. Women are taking leadership in making violence against women visible, and in addressing its causes, manifestations, and remedies.

THE EXTENT OF THE VIOLENCE

Violence against women is a problem that affects not only the poor or third world women; women in industrialised countries are also affected. Yet, even among industrialised countries, few researchers have undertaken the empirical studies that could provide a solid basis on which to map the true dimensions of the problem. In the developing world, with very few exceptions, statistics are even more scant. The seriousness of the problem should not be underestimated. When available, statistics powerfully document and make visible the pervasiveness and extent of violence against women globally.

Statistics from industrialised countries are disconcerting. Reports from Denmark indicate that 25 per cent of women cite violence as the reason for divorce. A 1984 study of urban victimisation in seven major Canadian cities found that 90 per cent of victims were women. One in four women in Canada can expect to be sexually assaulted at some point in their lives, one half of these before the age of seventeen (MacLeod, 1990).

While there are fewer studies in the third world, the pattern of gender violence there bears a remarkable similarity to that of advanced industrialised societies. Its manifestations may be culturally specific, but gender violence cuts across national boundaries, ideologies, classes, races and ethnic groups.

Within the context of the United Nations Decade for Women, many women and their representative organisations began to recognise the problem of violence against women. At all three world conferences on women, Mexico City (1975), Copenhagen (1980), and Nairobi (1985), and at the parallel non-governmental fora, women's advocates raised

15

the issue of gender violence and demanded special attention to the constraints it places on women's full participation in society.

HUMAN DEVELOPMENT AND VIOLENCE: A CONTRADICTION

When speaking of development, this paper relies on the approach adopted by the United Nations Development Programme (UNDP, 1990) in the Human Development Report (HDR). Reassessing the approaches that marked the three previous UN Development Decades, this document questions the ability of statistical indicators such as growth and national income to measure development adequately. Rather it suggests the need to focus on other aspects of development that provide more accurate and realistic indicators of human development: nutrition and health services, access to knowledge, secure livelihoods, decent working conditions, security against crime and physical violence, satisfying leisure time, and participation in the economic, cultural, and political activities of one's community. From this perspective, the goal of development is to create an environment that enables people to enjoy long, healthy, and creative lives.

Despite three decades of significant progress towards human development in the third world, particularly in relation to life expectancy, education and health, one has to examine cautiously the results from a cross-cultural gender perspective. Nowhere do females enjoy the same standards as males, and in some areas gaps have widened so considerably that one must question whether development attempts are intrinsically gendered to the disadvantage of females. As the HDR states: *'In most societies, women fare less well than men. As children they have less access to education and sometimes to food and health care. As adults they receive less education and training, work longer hours for lower incomes and have few property rights or none'* (UNDP, 1990).

Discrimination against females extends to every aspect of life. If women are fed less, have poorer health and less education than males, and their contribution to society's production and reproduction is underestimated, it is no wonder that wide gender gaps between males and females persist in human development indicators. Looking at development from a human centred gender perspective requires that development studies focus on women as a demographic category and that development indicators be recorded according to gender. In order for women to benefit from the development process, a fundamental

16

emphasis must be placed on increasing women's self confidence as well as their ability to participate in all aspects of society. Violence against women is in direct contradiction to securing human-centred development goals. It disrupts women's lives and denies them options. It erodes women's confidence and sense of self-esteem at every level, physically and psychologically. It destroys women's health, denies their human rights, and hinders their full participation in society. Where domestic violence keeps a woman from participating in a development project, or fear of sexual assault prevents her from taking a job or attending a public function, or force is used to deprive her of her earnings, development does not occur.

Women experience violence as a form of control that limits their ability to pursue options in almost every area of life from home to school, work-place, and most public spaces. Violence is used to control women's labour in both productive and reproductive capacities. For example, case studies of victims of domestic violence in Peru and of garment workers in the Mexican maquilas showed men beating their wives frequently to demand the income women had earned. (Vasquez and Tamayo, 1989; Dwyer and Bruce, 1990) Indonesian female workers returning to their villages complain of their helplessness in the face of harassment and sexual abuse; quite often their wages are withheld for months, preventing possibility of escape or resistance. In the Philippines, women workers in export oriented industries claim that male managers give female employees the choice of 'lay down or lay off' (AWRAN Report, 1985).

The socially constructed dependency of women on men is key to understanding women's vulnerability to violence. This dependency is frequently economic and results from various layers of sexist discrimination. First, much of women's work is unpaid labour at home and in the fields which is not valued by society nor calculated as part of the gross national product - the productive work of a nation. Second, even in paid jobs, women work longer hours for lower pay with fewer benefits and less security than men.

Female dependency extends to other areas as well, psychological, social and cultural. Women are trained to believe that their value is attached to the men in their lives - fathers, brothers, husbands, and sons. They are often socially ostracised if they displease or disobey these men. Women are socialised to associate their self-worth with the satisfaction of the needs and desires of others and thus are encouraged to blame themselves as inadequate or bad if men beat them. This socialisation process is reinforced by cultures in which a woman is constantly diminished, her sexuality commodified, her work and characteristics devalued, her identity shaped by an environment that reduces her to her biological functions. Yet, women are still blamed for 'causing' or deserving the abuse of men toward them.

Women's socio-economic and psychological dependency makes it difficult for them to leave situations of domestic violence or sexual harassment. Often in rural settings it is physically impossible; women literally have no place to go or the means to get away, and there are no services available to them. The Commonwealth Secretariat report on domestic violence cites the opinion of experts that a shelter or other safe refuge alternative is only possible in a city of at least 10,000 inhabitants.

But even in large urban settings, where it may be easier for women to leave abusive relationships, there is often nowhere to go, as illustrated by the links between domestic violence and homelessness. A shelter for homeless women in Boston reports that about ninety per cent of its occupants are victims of domestic violence (*The New York Times*, August 26, 1990), and New York City shelter workers note a similar trend. Australian sociologist, Robert Connell (1987) sees the lack of alternative housing as one of the reasons women stay in, or return to, violent marriages. Further, violence itself makes women become even more dependent. Studies from several countries find that the escalation of violence undermines women's self esteem and that their capacity to take action diminishes.

EFFECTS ON FAMILY, CHILDREN AND SOCIETY

Violence against women also affects the development and well being of children and families. A recent study on children of battered women in Canada reports post-traumatic stress, clinical dysfunction, behavioural and emotional disorders in children from violent homes (Jaffe, Wolfe, and Wilson, 1990). Some argue that children's socialisation into accepting or committing violence starts at home when they witness their father beating their mother and sometimes abusing them as well.

It seems increasingly clear that the best way to reduce infant mortality is through the education of women (White House Task Force on Infant Mortality Report, cited in *The New York Times*, August 12, 1990; Buvinic and Yudelman, 1989). The 1990 UNDP report underlines the high social dividend that comes with female literacy, as demonstrated by lower infant mortality rates, better family nutrition, reduced fertility and lower population growth. Other studies show a

18

connection between women's self-confidence and child mortality. Since the health and psychological well being of children is connected to the future development of a country, the gender violence implicit in disproportionate female illiteracy is clearly contrary to development. Improving women's self-confidence and education are therefore crucial investments that may have long lasting effects on children and the future of a nation.

Violence against women deprives society of the full participation of women in all aspects of development. As Lori Heise states: *'Female focused violence undermines widely held goals for economic and social development in the third world. The development community has come to realise that problems such as high fertility, deforestation and hunger cannot be solved without women's full participation. Yet women cannot lend their labour or creative ideas fully when they are burdened with the physical and psychological scars of violence'* (Heise 1989).

Many work hours are lost as a result of violence, not to speak of the costs of providing services to victims. In this we should take into account the work time lost by the victim herself, plus the work time of the police and others in the legal, medical, mental, health and social services. It is almost impossible to quantify the total costs of the problem given the limited information available on the extent of such violence. Violence in an environment in which public safety measures are inadequate and public transport unprotected, severely limits women's integration into the paid work force.

Violence against women is often a direct obstacle to women's participation in development projects. For example, in a Mexican project funded by the United Nations Development Fund for Women (UNIFEM) instances of wife battering increased with women's sense of empowerment through their participation. The project found that men perceived the growing empowerment of women as a threat to their control, and the beatings could be explained as an attempt to reverse this process of empowerment the women experienced in order to drive them away from the project. Similarly, a revolving fund project of the Working Women's Forum in Madras almost collapsed when the most articulate and energetic participants started to drop out because of increased incidents of domestic violence against them after they had joined. Faced with the same problems, the Association for the Development and Integration of Women (ADIM) in Lima succeeded in its work by initiating programmes that combined income-generating schemes with legal aid to battered wives and women abandoned by their partners (Buvinic and Yudelman, 1989).

Health is usually recognised as an important development issue. One of the clearest facts about violence against women is that it is detrimental to women's physical and mental health, including women's very survival. A 1989 report by the Surgeon General of the US, C. Everett Koop, affirms that battered women are four to five times more likely than non-battered women to require psychiatric treatment, and more likely to commit suicide. He reports that each year some one million women in the US are sufficiently injured to seek medical assistance at emergency rooms for injuries sustained through battering. Koop calls it *'an overwhelming moral, economic, and public health burden that our society can no longer bear'*. He demands a major response from governments at the national, state and community levels; legislators and city councils; police, prosecutors, judges and probation officers; health professions and educational institutions; the communications media; the church and clergy; non-governmental organisations, as well as *'international organisations that must demonstrate a clear recognition of the problem and provide the necessary leadership to us all'* (Koop, 1989).

UNDERSTANDING THE CAUSES OF VIOLENCE

Explaining why gender violence is so endemic is a complex endeavour best pursued as it relates to the question of prevention. There are innumerable theories ranging from biological and genetic explanations, to those which attribute causation to alcohol and toxic substance-abuse, poverty, socialisation and even women themselves (Commonwealth Secretariat, 1987). While some of these theories may contain a grain of truth, none of them justify violent behaviour and are better understood as co-factors that can concur with a violent situation. The major point here is to look at violence against women as learned behaviour, which can be changed. Gender violence can be prevented or, at least, substantially reduced if the social and political will exists to make this happen. This discussion is not intended as an abstract investigation into the origins of violence against women, but as an effort to see how understanding gender violence helps to create preventive strategies that go beyond the social service response.

A Peruvian study by Vasquez and Tamayo (1989) argues that causes of battery are many, including: unequal relations between men and women; the sexual hierarchy; domestic isolation of women with male figures as the final authority; early marriages before women have developed a sense of autonomy; the family as the sole institution that shapes women's identity; the representation of masculinity via the domination of women; poor communication in family conflicts; and the privatisation of conflict between men and women in a couple relationship. This suggests a number of important development objectives that might reduce such violence.

A Papua New Guinea study states: *'the essence of male violence against women is the sense of inadequacy, of vulnerability, of helplessness, of weakness, and of sheer naked fear that men inspire in women when they threaten or use violence against women. The use of brute force by men makes women feel inferior'.*

This suggests the crucial importance of building women's self confidence as a means of countering their vulnerability to violence.

The problem of violence against women is systemic and common to all societies. There are several levels on which women can take action in addressing the connections between gender violence and development. The overall question is how to make use of limited resources to support projects that take into account and challenge the limitations and constraints that violence places on women's full participation in development activities.

1. ACTION AT MULTIPLE PROGRAMME LEVELS

(a) Awareness of the obstacles posed by gender violence

(i) In the formulation and implementation phases of a development project, an awareness of forms of gender violence that are specific to certain cultures can help identify and overcome obstacles impeding women's participation.

(ii) Also at the formulation and implementation stages, sensitivity to situations in which changes in women's status makes them vulnerable to violence is essential. It is a cultural truism that change is threatening. Project activities might both seek to strengthen women's self-confidence and ability to defend themselves as well as reach out to men in the community, win their commitment to the change, and even change their expectations.

(iii) In personnel selection for the implementation stage, awareness of violence as an obstacle should be an important consideration. Project management requires not just technical skill, but an awareness of the larger environment and how it must be altered to facilitate women's full participation.

(iv) Gender violence which obstructs development, as well as measures which reduce women's vulnerability to violence need to be documented as they occur in the project cycle. It can be noted in periodic reporting, in staff monitoring visits, or in evaluations. The findings can be collected and analysed as part of lessons learned from project experience.

(b) *The integration of statistics on gender violence* into data collection, planning and training projects is central to the visibility and recognition of such violence as an obstacle to development.

(c) *Find sustainable ways of deterring gender violence.* Employing techniques or interventions that focus on, and deal with, violence.

(d) *Increase the capacity of women to identify and combat violence.* Projects which strengthen communication skills, raise women's awareness of possible actions, build management skills, teach self-defense, and strengthen women's organisations, at the same time contributing to enlarging women's capacity to address gender specific violence.

2. NON-PROGRAMMATIC STEPS

The international development community, and particularly women's agencies within that community, can undertake important changes that are not related to projects, and would not require additional expenditures beyond staff time. This involves making violence visible as a development issue in relation to many other themes. By disseminating reports of projects concerned with violence, women's advocates within the development community can highlight the impact of violence on programme activity.

Overall, development agencies and organisations addressing women in development must conduct their programme and project work with an increased sensitivity to the issue of violence, and the ways in which development itself brings forth new forms of gendered violence.

CONCLUSION

Attempts to integrate women into development are doomed to failure if they do not address the issue of violence against women. This paper has attempted to build the case for the international development community's support of projects that address the various manifestations of gender violence as legitimate development projects. It maintains that projects dealing with violence towards women are building blocks for a more comprehensive, empowering and therefore sustainable effort which will tap women's full participation in the development process.

The basic research for this paper was done under the sponsorship of the United Nations Development Fund for Women (UNIFEM).

REFERENCES for O'Connor, Bunch & Carrillo

Ashworth, G., *Of Violence and Violation: Women and Human Rights.* London: Change, 1989.
AWRAN Report, 1985.
Buvinic, M. and Yudelman, S.W., *Women, Poverty and Progress in the Third World.* New York: Foreign Policy Association, 1989.
Coliver, S., 'United Nations Machineries on Women's Rights: How Might They Better Help Women Whose Rights Are Being Violated?' in Lutz, Hannum, and Burke, eds., *New Directions in Human Rights.* Philadelphia: U. of Penn. Press, 1989.
Commonwealth Secretariat. Women and Development Programme, *Confronting Violence. A Manual for Commonwealth Action.* Prepared by J.F. Connors, 1987.
Connell, R.W., *Gender and Power.* Stanford: Stanford UP, 1987.
'The Convention on the Elimination of All Forms of Discrimination Against Women,' Summary of CEDAW prepared by the International Women's Rights Action Watch (IWRAW), Humphrey Institute of Public Affairs, Minneapolis, 1988.
'The Convention on the Elimination of All Forms of Discrimination Against Women; The Reporting Process - A Manual for Commonwealth Jurisdictions,' Commonwealth Secretariat, London, 1989.
Cook, R. J., *Bibliography: The International Right to Non-discrimination on the Basis of Sex.* Yale Journal of International Law 14:161, 1989.
Dwyer, S. and Bruce, J. eds., *A Home Divided.* Stanford: Stanford U, 1990.
Eisler, R., *Human Rights: Toward an Integrated Theory for Action.* Human Rights Quarterly, 9 (1987): 297.
Heise, L., *Crimes of Gender.* World Watch March-April 1989: 12-21.
Jaffe, Wolfe, Wilson, *Wife Battering in Canada: Re Vicious Circle.* Quebec: Government Publishing Centre, 1990.

Kellegher, P., Kellegher, C. and McCarthy, P., 'Patterns of Hostel Use in Dublin and the Implications for Accomodation Provision.' Focuspoint, Dublin, 1992.

Koop, Everett M.D., *Violence Against Women: A Global Problem.* Presentation by the Surgeon General of the U.S., Public Health Service, Washington D.C., 1989.

MacLeod, L., *Women and Environments.* Vol. 12, No. 1, Fall 89-Winter 1990.

Meyer, M., 'Oppression of Women and Refugee Status'. Unpublished report to NGO Forum, Nairobi, Kenya, 1985.

Patel, V., *In Search of Our Bodies: A Feminist Look at Women, Health and Reproduction in India.* Bombay: Shakti, 1987.

Portugal, A. M., *Cronica de Una Violacion Provocada?* Fempress especial *Contraviolencia,* Santiago, 1988.

Ravindran S., *Health Implications of Sex Discrimination in Childhood.* Geneva: World Health Organisation, 1986.

Rosca, N., Speech at Amnesty International, New York Regional Conference, 24 February, 1990.

Roy, M., *The Abusive Partner.* New York: New Liniu Press, 1982.

Sivard, R.L., *Women ... A World Survey.* Washington, D.C.: World Priorities, 1985.

Stark, E. and Flitchcraft, A., *Domestic Violence and Female Suicide Attempts.* Paper presented at the 107th annual meeting of the American Public Health Association. New York, November 1979.

Straus, N.A., Gelles, R. and Steinmetz, S.K., *Behind Closed Doors: Violence in the American Family.* New York: Doubleday, 1981.

Taylor, D., ed., *Women: A World Report.* A New Internationalist Book, Oxford: University Press, 1985.

United Nations. Centre for Social Development and Humanitarian Affairs. Division for the Advancement of Women, *Violence Against Women in the Family.* Prepared by J. F. Connors, 1989.

United Nations. *The Nairobi Forward-Looking Strategies for the Advancement of Women.* Adopted by the World Conference to review and Appraise the Achievements of the United Nations Decade for Women: Equality, Development and Peace. Nairobi, Kenya, 15-26 July 1985.

United Nations Development Programme, *Human Development Report 1990.* New York: Oxford UP, 1990.

Vasquez, R. y Tamayo, G., *Violencia y Legalidad.* Lima: Concytec, 1989.